THE WHITE CLIFFS
OF DOVER
SONGBOOK

Table Of Contents

Amor
(Amor, Amor, Amor)

English Lyric By Sunny Skylar
Music By Gabriel Ruiz
Spanish Lyric By Ricardo Lopez Mendez

American Patrol

By F.W. MEACHAM

Tempo di Marcia

ppp

(Patrol heard in the distance)

p

pp

(Patrol gradually approaches)

COLUMBIA, THE GEM OF THE OCEAN (Becket)

(Patrol passing)

✖   From here to ✖✖ on the following page, this number may be used separately.

(gradually retiring)

(Patrol disappearing)

(Gone)

dim. poco a poco sempre

And The Angels Sing

Words By Johnny Mercer
Music By Ziggy Elman

Sud-den-ly the set-ting is strange, I can see wa-ter and
moon-light beam-ing, sil-ver waves that break on some un-dis-cov-ered shore;
then sud-den-ly I see it all change, long win-ter nights with the
can-dles gleam-ing, thru it all your face that I a - dore.____ You

As Time Goes By

Words And Music By
HERMAN HUPFELD

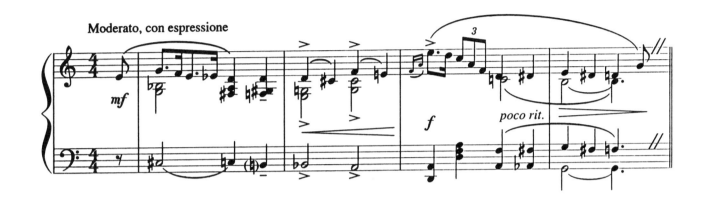

You must re-mem-ber this, a kiss is still a kiss, a sigh is just a sigh;

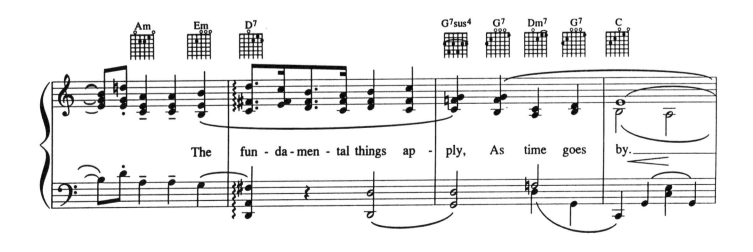

The fun-da-men-tal things ap-ply, As time goes by.

And when two lov - ers woo, they still say, "I love you," On

that you can re - ly; No mat - ter what the fu - ture

brings, As time goes by. Moon - light and love__ songs

mf - f *poco a poco cresc.*

nev - er out of date, Hearts full of pas - sion, jeal - ous - y and hate;

19

Begin The Beguine

Spanish Version By
MARIA GREVER

Words And Music By
COLE PORTER

tast - ed _____ And now when I hear peo-ple curse the chance that was wast - ed,
sar - nos _____ Y con la mas cruél mal-di - ción qui-so con-de - nar - nos ___

_____ I know but too well _____ what they mean; _____ So don't
Au - na so-le - dad _____ sin i - gual _____ Nun-ca ol -

let them be - gin _____ the Be - guine, _____ Let the
vi - des tu rit - - - mo sen - sual _____ Que la

love that was once a '- fire re-main an em - ber; _____ Let it
lla - ma de a-mor sin - ce - ro no se a - pa - ga _____ Ni el de-

Bei Mir Bist Du Schön

Music By Sholom Secunda
Original Lyric By Jacob Jacobs
English Version By Sammy Cahn and Saul Chapin

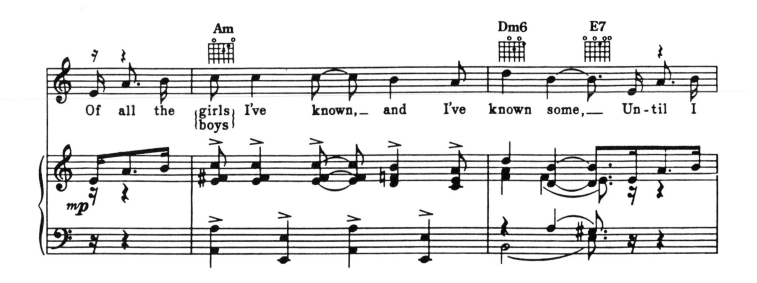

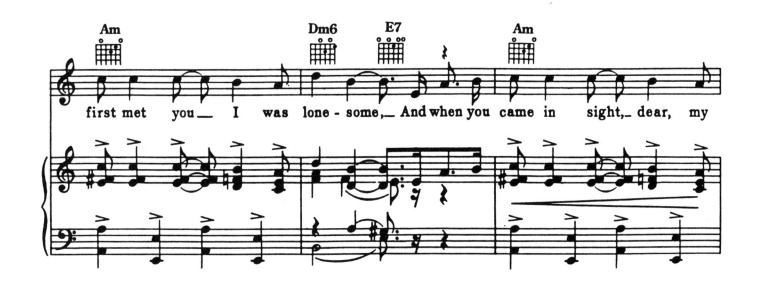

Blues In The Night

Words By Johnny Mercer
Music By Harold Arlen

By The Light Of The Silvery Moon

Music By Gus Edwards
Words By Edward Madden

Deep Purple
(Sombre Demijour)

Lyric By Mitchell Parish
Music By Peter DeRose
French Translation By Yvette Baruch

Candy

Words And Music By
MACK DAVID, JOAN WHITNEY
AND ALEX KRAMER

Dance With A Dolly
(With A Hole In Her Stockin')

Words And Music By
TERRY SHAND, JIMMY EATON AND MICKEY LEADER

I've got a se-cret, gon-na 'fess up to-night Gon-na dance by the light of the moon
Worked all day I'm gon-na scat out to-night And I won't be home un-til dawn Gon-na
Sweet-er than I've ev-er had be-fore Still I keep on cry-in' for more

DANCE WITH A DOL-LY with a hole in her stock-in' While our knees keep a-knock-in' and our

toes keep a-rock-in' DANCE WITH A DOL-LY with a hole in her stock-in' Dance by the light of the moon

sfz *(Optional music box effect in 2nd Chorus 8va)*

1 and 2 / 3

1.
2. She's

Gon-na dance by the light of the moon

pp (more softly)

Dance by the light of the moon By the light of the moon.

ppp (still more softly) broadly *mf* *f*

Dancing In The Dark

Words By Howard Dietz
Music By Arthur Schwartz

Dolores

Words By Frank Loesser
Music By Louis Alter

It was a sun-ny lit-tle, fun-ny lit-tle bor-der town___ Where on a moon-lit night I rode.___ And all the lo-cal guys were vo-cal-iz-ing up and down.___ Be-fore a cer-tain girl's a - bode.

throws! I would die to be with my Do - lo - res, Ay, ay, ay Do-

lo - res; I was made to ser - e - nade Do - lo - res, Cho - rus af - ter

cho - rus. Just im - ag - ine eyes like moon - rise____ A voice like

mu - sic,____ and lips like wine! What a break if I could make Do-

lo - res, Mine all mine. mine.____

I Can't Begin To Tell You

Words By Mack Gordon
Music By James V. Monaco

Don't Get Around Much Anymore

Words By Bob Russell
Music By Duke Ellington

Dream

Words And Music By Johnny Mercer

Slowly (with expression)

VERSE

Gm A7 D Dm7-5 G7 Cm

Get in touch with that sun-down fel-low,___ As he tip-toes a-cross the sand.

Cm7-5 F7 Bb D7 Gm C7 C9+5 C7 F9 F7-9

He's got a mil-lion kinds of star-dust, Pick your fav-'rite brand, and:

CHORUS (Slow tempo)

Bb6 A7 Bb

DREAM ___ when you're feel-in' blue, ___ DREAM ___

Bb Dm7 G7 Eb Ebm

___ that's the thing to do. ___ Just ___ watch the smoke-rings

57

Embraceable You

Words By IRA GERSHWIN
Music By GEORGE GERSHWIN

G.I. Jive

Words And Music By
JOHNNY MERCER

A Gal In Calico

Words By Leo Robin
Music By Arthur Schwartz

(Give Me)
Five Minutes More

Words By Sammy Cahn
Music By Jule Styne

I Cried For You

Words And Music By
Arthur Freed, Gus Arnheim
and Abe Lyman

used to be._____ Now I found two eyes just a lit-tle bit blu-er, I found a heart just a lit-tle bit tru-er. I Cried____ For You____ Now it's your turn to cry o-ver me._____ me.

I Don't Want To Walk Without You

Words By Frank Loesser
Music By Jule Styne

I Had The Craziest Dream

Words By Mack Gordon
Music By Harry Warren

When I'm a-wake—such a break——nev-er hap-ens. How long can a {guy—}{gal—} go on dream-ing?

—ing? If there's a chance—that you care,———— then, please say you do;—

(Ba-by) say it and make— my craz - i - est dream— come true.—

1.

2.

I'll Be Around

Words And Music By
ALEC WILDER

78

I've Got A Gal In Kalamazoo

Words By Mack Gordon
Music By Harry Warren

my, how she grew; _____ I ___ liked her looks,_ when I car-ried her books_ in Kal - a - ma - zoo,_ zoo, zoo,___ zoo, zoo.___ I'm gon-na send a wire,___ hop-pin' on a fly - er, leav - in' to - day.___ Am I dream - in'; I can hear her scream-in; "Hy -

a Mis-ter Jack-son" ev - 'ry-thing's O

Coda

hur-ry-ing to.___

I'm goin' to Mich-i-gan to see the sweet-est gal___ in Kal - a - ma -

1.

zoo.___

2.

zoo, zoo, zoo, zoo,

zoo!

Kal - a - ma - zoo!___

I'll Be Home For Christmas

Words By Kim Gannon
Music By Walter Kent

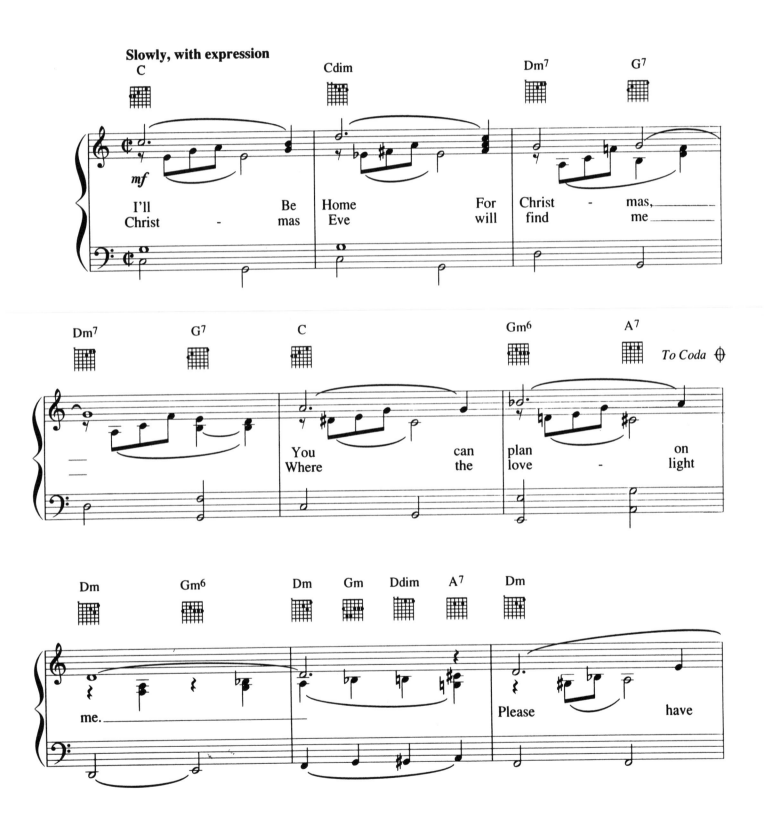

snow and mis - tle - toe And pre - sents on the tree.

D.C. al Coda

Coda

gleams.___ I'll Be Home For Christ - mas. If on - ly in my dreams.___

83

I've Heard That Song Before

Words By Sammy Cahn
Music By Jule Styne

84

It Had To Be You

Words By Gus Kahn
Music By Isham Jones

Jersey Bounce

Words By Buddy Feyne
Music By Bobby Plater, Tiny Bradshaw
And Edward Johnson

rhy-thm they play.___ It start-ed on Jour-nal Square,_____ and

some-bod-y heard it there,_____ he put it right on the air_____ and

now you hear it ev-'ry-where.___ Up-town ___ gave it new licks,___

down-town ___ add-ed some tricks,___ no town ___

It's Been A Long, Long Time

Words By Sammy Cahn
Music By Jule Styne

La Vie En Rose

Words By Mark David
Music By Louiguy
French Lyric By Edith Piaf

Mam'selle

Words By Mack Gordon
Music By Edmund Goulding

Love Letters

Words By Edward Heyman
Music By Victor Young

Moderately Slow with expression

The sky may be star-less the night may be moon-less, But deep in my heart there's a glow: _____ For deep in my heart I know that you love me. You love me, be-cause you told me so! _____

Refrain Love let-ters straight from your heart _____ Keep us so near _____ while a

The Marine's Hymn

ev - er   seen,_____   And we

glo - ry   in   the   ti -

tle   of   "U - nit - ed   States   Ma -

rine."_____   From the   rine."_____

Miss You

Words By Charlie Tobias And Harry Tobias
Music By Henry Tobias

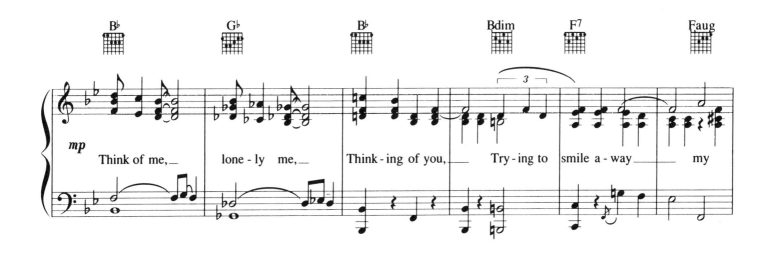

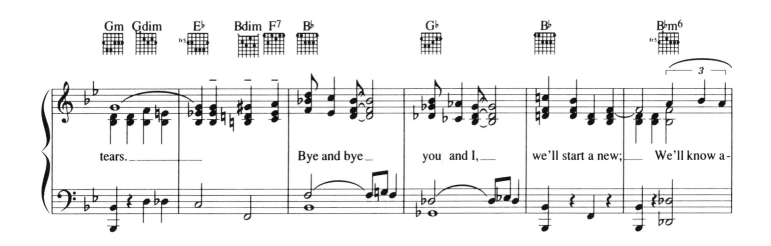

Moonlight Becomes You

Words By Johnny Burke
Music By James Van Heusen

Molto Moderato con espressione

Stand there just a mo-ment, dar-ling, let me catch my breath.

I've nev-er seen a pic-ture quite so love - ly.

How did you ev-er learn to look so love - ly?

My Ideal

Words By Leo Robin
Music By Richard A. Whiting and Newell Chase

My Dreams Are Getting Better All The Time

Words By MANN CURTIS
Music By VIC MIZZY

DREAMS ARE GET-TING BET-TER ALL THE TIME. — And what do you know she looked at me in a diff-'rent light! — MY DREAMS ARE GET-TING BET-TER ALL THE TIME. — To think that we were stran-gers A cou-ple of nights a-go, And tho' it's a dream, I nev-er dreamed she'd ev-er say "hel-lo". Oh, may-be to-night I'll hold her tight when the moon-beams shine, — MY DREAMS ARE GET-TING BET-TER ALL THE TIME. Well, TIME.

My Heart Tells Me

Words By MACK GORDON
Music By HARRY WARREN

My Prayer

Music By GEORGES BOULANGER
Lyric & Musical Adaptation By JIMMY KENNEDY

Oh! Look At Me Now

Words By John DeVries
Music By Joe Bushkin

I nev-er knew the tech-nique of kiss-in', I nev-er knew the thrill I could get from your touch, nev-er knew much, Oh! Look At Me Now.

I'm a new man, bet-ter than
(girl) in a whirl

Cas-a-no-va at his best.
nev-er knew love was like this.

With a new heart,

120

A Nightingale Sang In Berkeley Square

Lyric By ERIC MASCHWITZ
Music By MANNING SHERWIN

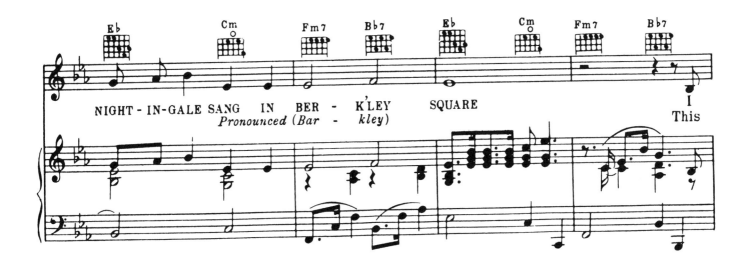

NIGHT-IN-GALE SANG IN BER - K'LEY SQUARE

Pronounced (Bar - kley)

This

may be right I may be wrong, But I'm per-fect-ly will-ing to swear That For
heart of mine beat loud and fast, Like a mer-ry-go-round in a fair

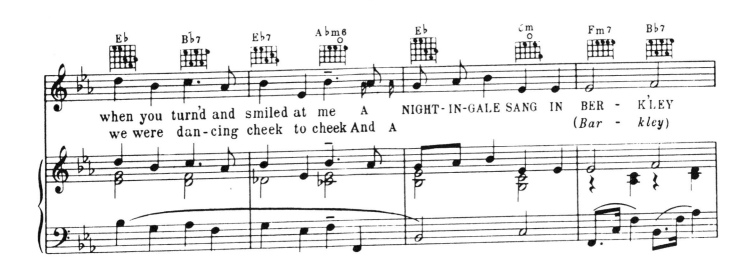

when you turn'd and smiled at me A NIGHT-IN-GALE SANG IN BER - K'LEY
we were dan-cing cheek to cheek And A

(Bar - kley)

SQUARE

The moon that lin-gered o-ver Lon-don town, Poor
When dawn came stealing up all gold and blue To

puz-zled moon, he wore a frown, How could he know we two were so in love The
in-ter-rupt our ren-dez-vous, I still re-mem-ber how you smiled and said "Was

whole darn world seemed up-side down The streets of town were paved with stars It was
that a dream or was it true?"Our home-ward step was just as light As the

such a ro-man-tic af-fair   And   as we kiss'd and said "good-night"   A
tap-dan-cing feet of As-taire   And   like an e-cho far a-way   A

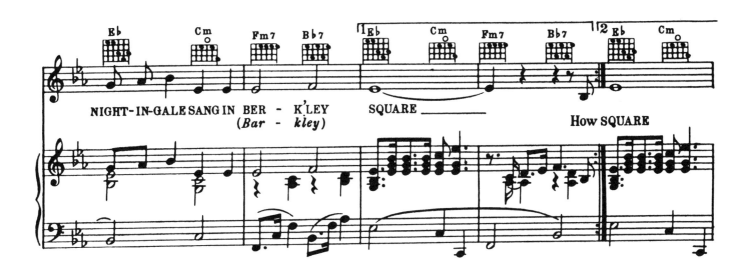

NIGHT-IN-GALE SANG IN BER - K'LEY   SQUARE _____
(Bar - kley)   How SQUARE

I know'cause I was there   That night in Ber-k'ley Square. _____
(Bar-k ley)
rall.

No Love, No Nothin'

Lyric By Leo Robin
Music By Harry Warren

Ole Buttermilk Sky

Lyric And Music By
HOAGY CARMICHAEL AND
JACK BROOKS

128

On The Atchison, Topeka
And The Santa Fe

Lyric By JOHNNY MERCER
Music By HARRY WARREN

got a list o' pas-sen-gers that's pret-ty big__ And they'll all want lifts to
Brown's Ho-tel,__ 'Cause lots o' them been trav-el-in' for quite a spell,__ All the
way from Phil-a - del-phi - ay,__ On The Atch-i - son, To-pe - ka And The
San-ta Fe.__ Do yuh San-ta Fe.__

(Single notes)..................
C D E G   E D C   A G   C B C Fdim Cdim   C

133

On The Sunny Side Of The Street

Music By Jimmy McHugh
Lyric By Dorothy Fields

One Dozen Roses

Words And Music By
ROGER LEWIS, COUNTRY WASHBURN,
DICK JURGENS AND WALTER DONOVAN

in an aw-ful hur-ry so don't ask me now to stop, I'm

go-ing to place an or-der in a lit-tle flow-er shop:

REFRAIN

Give me one doz-en ros-es Put my heart in be-side them And

send them to the one I love._____ She'll be

glad to re-ceive them And I know she'll be-lieve them That's

Over There

Words And Music By
GEORGE M. COHAN

Tempo di Marcia

John-nie get your gun, get your gun, get your gun, Take it on the
John-nie get your gun, get your gun, get your gun, John-nie show the

run, on the run, on the run; Hear them call-ing
Hun, you're a son-of-a-gun, Hoist the flag and

you and me; Ev-'ry son of lib-er-ty.
let her fly, Like true he-roes do or die.

Hur - ry right a - way, no de - lay, go to - day,
Make your dad - dy
Pack your lit - tle kit, show your grit, do your bit,
Sol - diers to the

glad, to have had such a lad,
Tell your sweet - heart
ranks from the towns and the tanks,
Make your moth - er

not to pine, To be proud her boy's in line.
proud of you, And to lib - er - ty be true.

Chorus *March Tempo*

O - ver there, ___ o - ver there, ___ Send the word, send the word o - ver

141

Paper Doll

By Johnny S. Black

VERSE

I guess I've had a mil-lion dolls or more, I guess I've played the doll game o'er and o'er, I just quar-reled with Sue,— That's why I'm blue;— She's gone a-way and left me just like all dolls do. I'll tell you boys it's tough to be a-lone And it's

Peg O' My Heart

Words By Alfred Bryan
Music By Fred Fischer

145

need you much more— than I can say,_____ I know I'm aim-ing high__ But a
love her, I love__ her fond and true,_____ And her heart fond-ly sighs,__ As I

dream-er can try__ So why can't I_____ Just dream and sigh my love song!
sing to her eyes,__ Her eyes of blue,_____ Sweet eyes of blue, my dar-ling!

Slowly

Refrain:

Peg O' My Heart _____ I love you, Don't let us part, __
Peg O' My Heart _____ I love you, We'll nev-er part, __

mp - mf

I love you, I al-ways knew.__ It would be you, __
I love you, Dear lit-tle girl,__ Sweet lit-tle girl, __

Pennsylvania 6-5000

Lyric By Carl Sigman
Music By Jerry Gray

150

Sentimental Journey

Words And Music By
BUD GREEN, LES BROWN AND BEN HOMER

Very slowly

Verse

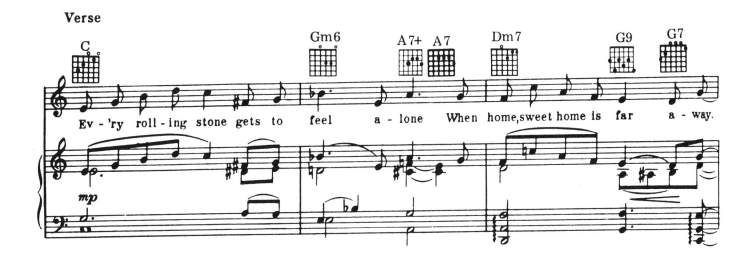

Ev-'ry roll-ing stone gets to feel a-lone When home, sweet home is far a-way.

I'm a roll-ing stone who's been so a-lone Un-til to-day.

I'll be wait-in' up for Heav-en, Count-in' ev-'ry mile of rail-road track that takes me back.

Nev - er thought my heart could be so "yearn-y." Why did I de - cide to roam?

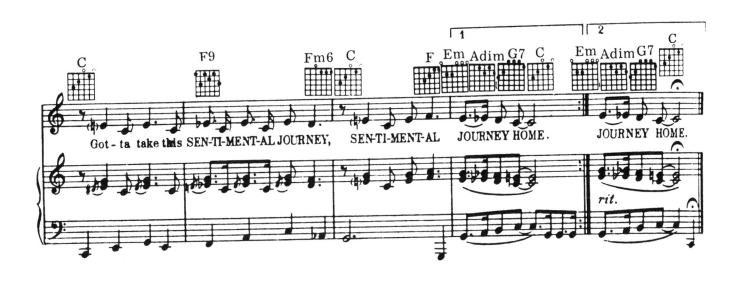

Got - ta take this SEN-TI-MENT-AL JOURNEY, SEN-TI-MENT-AL JOURNEY HOME. JOURNEY HOME.

Prisoner Of Love

Words And Music By
LEO ROBIN, CLARENCE GASKILL
AND RUSS COLUMBO

154

wait now, From one who's mas-ter of my Fate now;

I can't es-cape, for it's too late now, I'm just a pris'-ner of

love. What's the good of my car-ing, if some-one is shar-ing Those

arms with me? Al-though {he / she} has an-oth-er, I

157

Racing With The Moon

Words By Vaughn Monroe and Pauline Pope
Music By Johnny Watson

Remember Pearl Harbor

Words And Music By
DON REID AND SAMMY KAYE

Verse: His-to-ry ___ in ev-'ry cen-tu-ry ___ re-cords an act that lives for-e-ver-more. ___ We'll re-call, ___ as in-to line we fall, ___ the thing that hap-pened on Ha-wa-ii's shore. ___

Chorus: Let's RE-MEM-BER ___ PEARL HAR-BOR ___ As we go to

Rum And Coca-Cola

Lyric By Morey Amsterdam
Additional Lyric By Al Stillman
Music By Jeri Sullavan and Paul Baron

Saturday Night
(Is The Loneliest Night In The Week)

Words By Sammy Cahn
Music By Jule Styne

Sun-day night at all _____ 'cause thats the night friends come to call _ And

Mon-day to Fri - day go fast _____ and an - oth er week is past,_ But

SAT-UR-DAY NIGHT is the lone _ li est night in the week,_____ I sing the

song that I sang_ for the mem - 'ries I u - sual-ly seek. _____ Un-til I

hear you at the door _____ Un til you're in my arms once more_ SAT-UR-DAY NIGHT is the lone-

_ li-est night in the week. _____

Seems Like Old Times

Words And Music By
CARMEN LOMBARDO AND JOHN JACOB LOEB

September Song

Words By Maxwell Anderson
Music By Kurt Weill

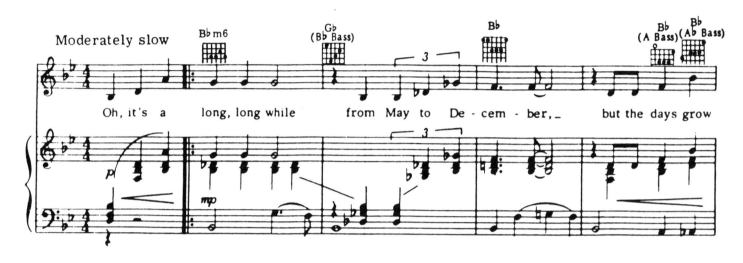

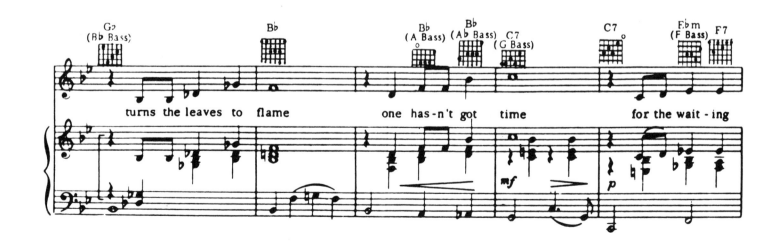

game. _____ Oh, the days dwin-dle down _____ to a

pre-cious few, _____ Sep-tem-ber, _____ No-vem-ber!

And these few pre-cious days I'll spend with you, These pre-cious

days I'll spend with you. Oh, it's a you. _____

Serenade In Blue

Words By Mack Gordon
Music By Harry Warren

like the theme of some for-got-ten mel - - o - dy

in the al - bum of my mem-o - ry, ———— Ser - e - nade ——— In

Blue. It seems like on - ly yes-ter-day, a small ca-fe, a crowd-ed floor, and

as we dance the night a-way, I hear you say, "For-ev-er more," and then the song be-came a sigh, for-

ev - er - more be-came good-bye, but you re-mained in my heart._____ So

tell me dar - ling, is there still a spark, _____ or on - ly lone - ly ash - es of the

flame we knew; should I go on whis - tling in the dark? _____ Ser - e-nade _____

In Blue. _____ Blue. _____

Sleepy Time Gal

Words By Joseph Reed Alden and Raymond B. Egan
Music By Ange Lorenzo and Richard A. Whiting

Would-n't it be a change for you and me to stay at home once in a while?
Would-n't it be a pleas-ant sight to see a kitch-en-ette on-ly for you?

We cab-a-ret un-til the break of day, I'll bet we've danced man-y a mile.
Would-n't it be a pleas-ant sight to see, A ta-ble set on-ly for two?

I'd like to see a mov-ie once more, They don't keep peo-ple stay-in up un-til four.
I'll get a big Vic-tro-la and then, We'll start in danc-ing ev-'ry new dance a-gain,

Some Sunday Morning

Words By Ted Koehler
Music By M.K. Jerome and Ray Heindorf

Somebody Else Is Taking My Place

Words And Music By
Dick Howard, Bob Ellsworth and Russ Morgan

Slowly *(with expression)*

Some-bod-y else is tak-ing my place

Some-bod-y else now shares your em-brace While I am

try-ing To keep from cry-ing You go a-round with a

Something To Remember You By

Words By
HOWARD DIETZ

Music By
ARTHUR SCHWARTZ

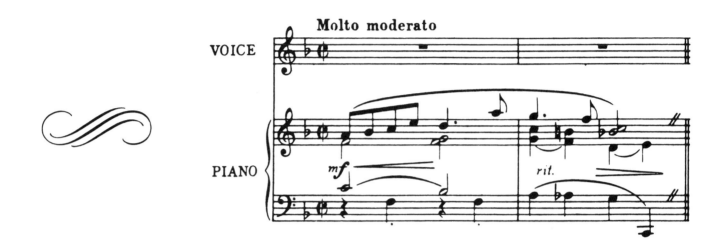

Straighten Up And Fly Right

Words And Music By
Nat "King" Cole and Irving Mills

chok-in' me,— Re-lease your holt and I will set you free," The mon-key looked the buz-zard right

dead in the eye, And said,"Your sto-ry's so touch-ing, it sounds just like a lie."

STRAIGH-TEN UP AND FLY— RIGHT!— Straigh-ten up and stay— right.—

STRAIGH-TEN UP AND FLY— RIGHT!— Cool—down, Pa-pa, don't you blow your top.— blow your top.—

Star Dust

Lyric By Mitchell Parish
Music By Hoagy Carmichael

and I am once a-gain with you; ___ when our love was new

and each kiss an in-spir-a - tion, ___ but that was long a-go: now

my con-so-la - tion is in the star dust of a song. Be -

side a gar-den wall, when stars are bright, you are in my arms. The

night - in - gale tells his fair - y tale of par - a - dise where ros - es

grew. _____ Tho' I dream in vain, _____ in my heart it will re -

main: My star dust mel - o - dy, _____ the mem - o - ry of love's re -

frain. Some-times I frain. _____

Symphony

Words By Andre Tabet and Roger Bernstein
American Version By Jack Lawrence
Music By Alex Alstone

Sing-ing vi - o - lins start in my heart.

Then you speak____ The mel - o - dy seems to rise____

Then you sigh,____ It sighs and it soft - ly dies,____

Sym-pho - ny____ sing to me____

191

Together

Words And Music By B.G. DeSylva,
Lew Brown and Ray Henderson

Tempo di Waltz moderato

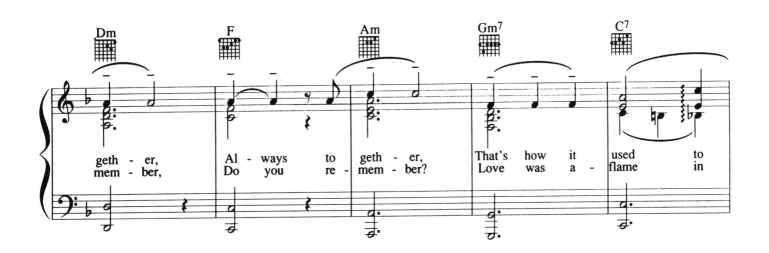

195

There Goes That Song Again

Words By Sammy Cahn
Music By Jule Styne

(There'll Be Blue Birds Over)
The White Cliffs Of Dover

Words By Nat Burton
Music By Walter Kent

Twilight Time

Words By Buck Ram
Music By Morty Nevins and Al Nevins

We Did It Before
And We Can Do It Again

Words And Music By
CLIFF FRIEND AND CHARLIE TOBIAS

202

REFRAIN

WE DID IT BE - FORE and we can do it a - gain and
WE DID IT BE - FORE and we can do it a - gain and

we will do it a - gain,_____ We've got a heck of a
we will do it a - gain,_____ We know we're right and we

job to do but you can bet that we'll see it thru.
al - so know that gang - ster - is - m has got to go.

WE DID IT BE - FORE and we can do it a - gain and
WE DID IT BE - FORE and we can do it a - gain and

We Three
(My Echo, My Shadow and Me)

Words And Music By
Dick Robertson, Nelson Cogane and Sammy Mysels

Here we go a-gain just rem-i-nisc-ing, ___ Dream-ing of

yes-ter-day, ___ And the joys we're miss - ing.

silver-y moon-light that shines a-bove? ___ I walk with my shad-ow, I

talk with my ech-o, But where is the one I love? WE THREE, we'll wait for

you, Ev-en 'till e-ter-ni-ty, My Ech-o,___ My

Shad-ow___ And Me. WE Me.

Who Wouldn't Love You

Words By Bill Carey
Music By Carl Fischer

What Do You Do In The Infantry?

By Frank Loesser

what do you do in the In - fan - try? You march, you march, you march!

What do you do in the In - fan - try? You hike, you hike, you hike.

What do you get in the In - fan - try? A left and right o - blique._____ The
(pronounced O-blike)

son - of - a - gun in the Sig - nal Corps is trav - el - ing on a bike,_____ And

You Made Me Love You

Words By Joe McCarthy
Music By James V. Monaco

You'll Never Know

Words By Mack Gordon
Music By Harry Warren

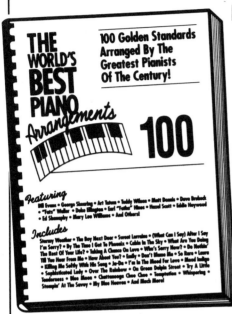